OUT OF THE ORDINARY

Kenneth Steven

All best wishes,

Kenneth Steven

SAINT ANDREW PRESS

First published in 2020 by
SAINT ANDREW PRESS
121 George Street
Edinburgh EH2 4YN

ISBN 978 1 80083 005 9

Poems in *Out of the Ordinary* have been published by *Scintilla*,
Life and Work, *The Furrow* (Ireland), *Northwords Now* and *Sojourners* (US).
'The Holy Isle' was broadcast on BBC Radio 3, and part of the
'Easter' sequence was used in the service from King's on BBC2.
'Parts V and IX of the Easter sequence first appeared in the collection
Evensong (SPCK, 2011) and are reproduced here by permission.

British Library Cataloguing in Publication Data
A catalogue record for this book is available from the British Library.

Typeset by Mary Matthews

Printed in the United Kingdom by CPI Group (UK) Ltd

CONTENTS

Knowledge	1
Kyrie	2
Newborn	3
Cairngorm	4
At Pluscarden Abbey	5
Sabbath	6
Sight	7
The Holy Isle	8
Out of the Ordinary	9
Next Morning	10
Dad	11
The Ross	12
The Book of Kells	13
The Abbey	14
Understanding	15
Always September	16
The St Kilda Wind	17
Little Wonder	18
Gift	19
Necropolis	20
Pasternak	21
Lost	22
The Damsons	23
Together	24
Place	25
Dan	26

Christmas:
   The Star   27
   The Innkeeper's Wife   28
   Nativity   29
The Glen   30
Swallows   31
Crime and Punishment   32
Search   33
The Truth   34
Brine   35
The Twelfth   36
Mother   37
Flanders   38
Boxing Day   39
Spoutwells   40
The Swans   41
The Two   42
Autumn   43
Nothing   44
Learning   45
Easter: I–X   46-57
Way   58

To Marion Faulds,
Morag Pepper and Jim Campbell,
in grateful thanks for friendship

KNOWLEDGE

Sometimes everything is not wrong
and the autumn morning
blues into all that was ever meant –
the trees coppered by the water
and the geese ragged in the low sky.
There is no need to fear for time stands
still and mirrored in the loch's clear sheen.

And we who are made of time
wait by windows and know
we have escaped into a place
where clocks and watches do not count
and a light that autumns always had
is ours alone.

KYRIE

When the beautiful world spread her branches
over and above your head
the sun curled the edges of your smile,
brought drops of shining when the moonlight fell
across the wide open land of your hands.

How tender the tomorrows in your gentle feet;
how fragile their miles that must not lose
nor fail the nakedness of touch, of breath –
mending the web's thread, healing her skin.

In time you will put your life before the canon
and your hand where the trees are cut,
pouring long selfless love back for the wound
that bled you, opened out your world
when first your feet stood made below the stars.

NEWBORN

Just after midnight, a foal
born to the island;
upright now in the morning,
sure already of the earth.

Welcomed down here
into the soar and swoop of swallows,
the good June sun –
nestled by the windswept grass.

A star had fallen from the sky,
sand-white and silked about the edges;
half-surprised by his own safe landing,
all ready to begin becoming.

CAIRNGORM

I'd climb all day until I reached the roof –
a granite plateau made of moss and snow.
I'd bring no water, rather stretch down deep
through pools of clear and freezing cold to find
and fill my thirst. I'd pitch my tent and wait
until the full moon rose on midnight, turned
each shard and fleck of stone to silver-white,
as deer clicked out across the brittle rim
so not another thing might be alive
until the very edges of the sky.
I'd waken, strange, and see the newborn sun
had made my face pure amber in the dawn.

AT PLUSCARDEN ABBEY

Only once have I stood beneath a tree
holding my breath to hear an owl.
Its voice was ragged; tattered at the edges –
a call that carried wide across the woods
in the still blue warmth that August dusk.
And everywhere along the valley's edge
came callings of other owls until I thought
they talked to one another, voices
almost like strange lamps strung out
into the night over a darkened sea.
I held my breath and heard their woven calls
as the moon rose whole and huge above the hills.

SABBATH

That day the air was different.
The fields lay under the sky
not breathing; the sun above them
broke like a glass vase, spilled bits of light
over the long dark edge of the moor.

The farms lay in their own lands
as if somehow in a vast cathedral, still
in the presence of their creator.

No tractors rambled out across the Easter acres;
no teenage cars, thudding with rock and roll,
slammed along the back roads.
Only a few lapwings rose and swivelled,
their high song carrying eerily
in a wind, an endless wind.

Through the window I saw them going to church –
black crows, their suits and hats
immaculate. The rain slanted
from a bruise of cloud; the women scuttled
fastening flapping hats to heads
with Bibled hands.

I went outside
into the worshipping of the larks,
the thanksgiving of the spring.

SIGHT

The strangeness of that sudden rumble
coming from nowhere yesterday late.
I ran out and stood watching
the faraway threatening skies,
but around us an eerie brightness –
the stillness that comes before storm.
The first flicker – a blink of silver,
seconds later the answering thunder.
I went in and watched from the window,
looked out and into the distance –
the lochan like a light blue stone
brooched in the tweed of the moorland.
The swans in the mirrored water,
so impossibly white to the eyes –
like the remains of snow after winter,
carvings that dipped and bent;
together yet ever themselves –
heads stretching into the west,
into the rain that came from the silence,
the veil that swallowed the day.

THE HOLY ISLE

What was the point of going there
except to be apart, to leave behind
the babble of the voices that could never know
how many angels there were dancing on a pin.
This was beyond: a place where silence spoke –
a few fields scattered in between the rocks,
a well of water for the quenching of their thirst
and beehive cells for shelter come the dark.
These were the simple things that made their lives.
What mattered more was breaking through
from out of solitude and quiet, now and then,
into somewhere else; a realm
where they could know the voice of God,
that took them from the ordinary
into a deeper light and out of time.

OUT OF THE ORDINARY

out of the ordinary comes love
big enough to build a house that's open
to those who yearn that God might enter in,
and breathe light through the dark that we have made

out of the ordinary love that spreads
wide her arms, embracing those
left by the side of the road, who've heard
time after time they are not good enough

out of the ordinary God that comes
into life not to kill joy but to kindle it, a God
who's crossed out all our wrongs and welcomes us
back home with happiness,
bigger than we ever could believe

NEXT MORNING

The lilies lie bruised on the pond,
their eyes open to the light.

Floodwater in blue and white stretches
along the length of the land.

Above us
swallows perform miracles without thinking;

do things with sky
we cannot begin to imagine.

Last night thunder padded above us
like an angry grandfather;

today he has no memory of anything
but smiles, reaches out an old hand.

DAD

On big blue days you took me there
to the crown of the hill, the strong sun
slanting my eyes with its soreness,
the wind tugging like a puppy at the car
rocking us on the last grass plateau.
And the kite rippled up into the air,
gusting beyond the ends of my arms;
you holding me down, until suddenly
I wished I could lose my footing and fall
upwards into the white-blue spiralling of the sky
and fly. But you held me; the weight of your hand
kept my shoulders down and sure and safe.
And that was what you were, always,
when I wanted to fight and fly and run –
the hand that held me steady,
that kept me from being blown away,
that made me wait till the storm was over.
I've been through all the boxes in the attic,
but the kite is gone, isn't there –
like you, it's blown away.

THE ROSS

The year's door shuts. The last red berries fall
and leave the rowan branches bare and dark
when in the night the wind begins to lift.
The sea booms white and huge;
a ledge of snow hallows the ben's bare head. And then
it's still: stars breathe the blue-black sky like brine.
The only colour left next day is grey
except when sudden sunlight comes to glow
the granite headland out across the sound,
firing the rubbled rock a bonfire orange bright
so all there is to do is stand and watch
as though some miracle were being born
and God was speaking through the stone once more –
that strange and still small voice of calm alive.

THE BOOK OF KELLS

Here in the Hebrides, out in a place
that was the middle of it all –
a nook and cranny of the west, frightened by Vikings –
a cloister where prayers scuffed and smoothed the stone.
They made these sacred pages to outlast them;
a forest full of the song of Christ,
each frond an honouring of the glory of their time –
in sapphire, crimson, gold.

THE ABBEY

That evening when I reached the abbey
it seemed so bare: the absence
of everything that I had left behind.
I saw bare floor, hard bed, white walls.
I sat and wondered why I was there
and then looked out the window, glimpsed
the flickering of swallows. An advent calendar window,
the kind you opened once with careful hands,
to find a blue sky full of stars above a stable.

Except that this was at the end of long, long summer.
I looked out now and saw the swallows
weaving tapestries from air
above the silence of the garden and the trees.
I opened wide the window as though to be among them,
somehow to touch their wings –
half a hundred of them, maybe more:
I closed my eyes and knew why I was there.

UNDERSTANDING

That afternoon I was in the garden
down on my knees, hacking at hard earth.
In the middle of my own noise I heard something,
looked up to listen, wondering if it was the main road –
the whine of motorcycles, the silver slush of cars –
till I realised it must be up above me
in the still dizziness of the April air,
a whole *huzz* of bumble bees that rambled
in the snowy softness of the cherry blossom crown,
and as the hills hung in the blue mist
I stopped to listen, on my knees,
to their held note, their woven hum.

ALWAYS SEPTEMBER

I whirred deep lanes like flickering tunnels;
caught glimpses of the light that swept the fields,
and shadows big as ships.
Sometimes I splayed the bicycle down,
still whirring; opened the door of the woods to pad
deep into glades made of secret greens –
imagined I'd walked into a book of tales
all still untold. I came home slow, the skies
a blue that had no name.
And when I woke next day
the first frost breathed the dawn.

THE ST KILDA WIND

A hundred miles west of sanity
St Kilda lies like the wreck of a dragon
crashed into Atlantic waves.

A few bones of bare rock, ungreened;
only a million seabirds wheeling the white stacks,
the air sweet with their stink.

Yet how many hundred years
a huddle of humanity clung to these rocks,
spindling the cliffs with their homemade ropes
to bring back baskets of birds.

Their whole lives chased by wind;
not a breeze, not even a gusting,
but a full-blown gale of wind –
everywhere they went and each new day.

They learned to live with it,
their faces windswept
till it was woven through them.

How strange in 1930
when they were beaten in the end
and a boat brought them back to the mainland.

How strange the quiet must have seemed to them;
how it must have kept awake their nights;
how they must have had to learn to walk again
unheld by weather – to tightrope the silence,
the tree-lined boredom of our towns.

As the ghosts of white birds
still wheeled and clamoured their heads –
held in the hands of the wind.

LITTLE WONDER

I come back from Craighouse
on the school bus. Children get out
into the wild sunlight of the March day,
wave goodbye at the top of nowhere roads,
diminish in the wing mirror's memory.

The bus hums on towards the ferry;
I peer out on to the final miles, wanting to hold
the huge light blowing the shale-grey shoulders
of these mountains old as earth.
I catch moments of birds,
sudden sunlight, the shudder of the cloud –
all passing and all slipping soon away.

And I realise this is what we are:
watchers of the world for just a little,
hands open for a few precious seconds of the light
to keep and hold for ever.

GIFT

Take nothing with you but your shoes.
The path is easy, and once the river opens
into the cupped hands of a pool
swim without fear of being seen.
Walk softly, so sometimes you are surprised
by the full sweetness of birdsong.
The cabin is never locked; anything that's taken
was needed more by someone else.
There is no need of artificial light:
a few candles are enough to warm the dark.
Before you sleep, go out into the silence of the stars
and listen to nothing but the hugeness of the night.

NECROPOLIS

The slow shriek of the gate clangs –
I stand beyond the *swish-swish* of the cars,
the heart's drum calm at last.

The sun emerging like a hedgehog from the mist,
trees sculpted out of silence;
wintered in the distance, made of grey.

Breeze comes and ruffles through the ditches;
the sun is snowballed under cloud
as rain in bits and pieces stings.

Some stones are toppled: the names of those beneath
all smooth and rubbed away –
they do not matter any more, for no-one comes

to crouch down close beside with candles,
to wait for dawn with them and pray
their souls have passed into a better light.

Homeless men creep here instead like moles
and cuddle up beneath the lintels, snug –
the living seeking succour from the dead.

They curl inside these caves, carve out a quiet
far from screaming tenements and teeming streets
to sleep untroubled through the hours of dark.

And in the morning, if they are blessed,
the deer come close to scent their breath
and rusty-furred the fox-cubs yap and scrabble.

This is a place made somehow more alive
than all the world beyond.

PASTERNAK

Staring into the mirror
he caught the reflection that haunted always –

Stalin, looking unblinking
at each thought and every deed.

The admissions of guilt, the confessions;
the show trials he saw through the walls,

so the writer's words poured from the pen
like blood, like shrieks on paper.

The staircase echoed with the footsteps
of those who waited and watched

and at night, alone in the darkness,
he listened for the sound of the car

that might take him away at last –
till he wished they would break down the door

so he could answer the questions he'd learned
by heart from the very start.

LOST

a forest clearing where the sun
slants inwards on the stems of trees
and a wood wasp is the only thing
that sings the silence sweet

for I know well that there are times
when lost inside a forest is
not bad but beautiful, when this
is almost then akin

to being deep inside a gem of green
where light and shadow only play
and nothing else is true except
the secrecy of somewhere strange

to be a child again instead
unmapped and free outwith the world
and wait there for the dark to rise –
in honeycombs of stars and stars

THE DAMSONS

All summer they are deep green,
clenched fists hidden in the heights;
maddeningly hard to so much as glimpse,
when the wind comes and whelms the canopy of leaves.

Only after everything else is gathered are they there:
blue-sheened, beautiful, the colour of bruises
softened by long days of autumn rain.

Only then do I remember them, go out with a long stick,
nudge them from their roosts until they thump
one by one into the mud.

And yet there's more than that,
as I drop the stick back down into the grass
and the last light goldens all the woods and hills,
that last long hour before the dark.

TOGETHER

Something about going together
out into the night, through stillness –
a darkness mothed with quiet.
And how she takes his hand in hers
and points to a sky all breathed with stars,
and there the first one falling in a silver streak.
Her eyes come back to him and he remembers
how they have journeyed through the winters
to find this place of safety now at last.

He looks with her and sees the stars
come falling over one another down into their night
so soft and silent, beautiful bright trails;
some scratches on the sky, some strokes of chalk.
He holds the warmth of her, that hand
with which she's held his life together
and asks that they might know
a path that's somehow just the same
of beauty and of light.

PLACE

The middle of the night is a strange and shoeless place;
stormy with moonlight, the roads like empty rivers
gullied and dug out of silver. The huge silence
is eerie, yet empty and absent of ghosts.
It is a place where the telephone stands dead;
where the sleepless make their long journey
like climbers among barren rocks, slow hour by hour
till the blessed hope of light at last –
the green eye of Venus low above the hills,
and the first long slush of a car's path into dawn.

DAN

The telephone crying and crying,
full of the news of your death.
Yet hadn't you really been dying
since school days when they started searching
for the piece of your mind that was missing?

Nothing but peace of mind
what you searched for the next forty years
down white corridors in patient rooms waiting.
You found it perhaps for a moment
in the dizziness of a new cigarette,
at the bottom of another glass.

And now you've found it in death
on an early morning of mist
when the river you grew up beside
is fleeced like a flowing collie,
the trees caught between orange and gold.

What can they speak at your funeral
but soft words like the petals of candles?
They don't know where you once went wrong
any more than the medical men
who found not answers but questions.

I'll remember the you who was happy,
whose eyes still laughed with the light.
We both had the whole world ahead:
one of us went on without stopping,
the other left for ever behind.

CHRISTMAS

The Star

The town was tight as a drum with strangers;
the nights sweaty with people and their flocks.
Then, that night, the star came;
bits of silver sprinkled over hills,
and everything else seemed suddenly dark.

I remember trying to sleep and cracklings of light
sparking the room, a strange and silent lightning.
I suppose in the end we forgot to remember –
the market was roaring, and there was another silver
to be made by the bucket-load. The star got lost
behind a host of other things.

But that one night I came home another way,
my head all smooth with wine.
A light in a stable; the gold of faces looking out at me
as in a painting. They had nothing;
I have houses, women, land –
yet for a second, one single moment,
I felt a different kind of emptiness,
was sure that they had more than I would ever know.

They're gone now. The town is just the same
and yet I feel their absence even yet –
a star is keeping me awake.

The Innkeeper's Wife

I reckon it was the girl,
not more than fourteen. Those eyes.

Something made him stop his talk,
hoist down the lantern and mutter out with them.

And that was one sour night –
dust and wind, things banging;

folk still wandering the town like ghosts
and hammering the doors.

Our place was loud with coins and drink,
and this was long past midnight.

It wasn't him that came back somehow;
that's all I'll say, I can't explain.

As though he'd seen something;
as though his eyes were somewhere else.

The first spear of light next day and he was out
with that fresh pail of milk –

and he would not say where he was going.

Nativity

When the miracle happened it was not
with bright light or fire –
but a farm door with the thick smell of sheep
and wind tugging at the shutters.

There was no sign the world had changed for ever
or that God had taken place;
just a child crying softly in a corner,
and the door open, for those who came to find.

THE GLEN

However many Februarys ago
we drove up and out of town
into the glen, a thousand feet above
to straggled farms half-hidden here and there.

We opened the car doors:
the whole air hallowed with birdsong –
the first daffodils struggling the wind,
a field of fading snow.

The light coming and going,
blown out of nowhere so a certain place
was lit and for a moment held, all bright and gold,
before everything was swept away once more.

It felt as though we'd somehow found
a beautiful beyond, left still alive;
unbroken by the roads and everything below –
like a bird's egg – shining, blue and precious.

SWALLOWS

Every summer dusk they come
these silky-soft black shapes
that flit and nip the stillness of the light
above the loch that lies unmoving grey;
the air all smudged with midges
dancing in a thousand Highland jigs.
The swallows dip and curve, they smooth the sky
in silent shadows weaving back and forth.
I stand and watch their patterns through the dusk,
the day's breath held; no single sound alive,
and think of all the thousand miles
that lie still mapped inside each swallow's flight,
these fluttering things that come in clouds in spring,
that sweep around our lives all summer long
and then fly back the length of Africa again.
I think of how our living on this gentle earth
is swallow-light, so delicately fine;
I wonder what we'd be bereft of birds like this
that touch and bless the edges of the heart.

CRIME AND PUNISHMENT

They had to be there by a quarter to six, she said.
They went out, the two of them,
that small hand in the big hand,
into the wet September day,
started across the park, running.
And I saw them as though in slow motion,
heard the soundlessness of the mother's words,
her little girl's pigtails flying behind.
I watched them through splintering rain, diminishing,
and thought of the prison they were visiting;
wondered why he was there, how often they came.
The rain on the glass melted them,
broke them into pieces, washed them away;
the hugeness of the prison walls against them –
one yellow anorak and one red,
smaller and smaller into the distance –
nothing changed at all
since Tolstoy, since Hardy, since Dostoevsky.

THE SEARCH

Who was it who decreed
we must find God
through the hard labour of hunger
or years of rocky islands?

Why should God not also be
found listening in a simple glade
where morning is being born
in the soft calling of birds?

THE TRUTH

The light is like deep water:
I cannot sleep but feel the ship that is the house
rise up and fall again, the whole world made of blue –
the sea, the sky, the light. The curtains bloom
and fill with dry wind in a night that won't grow dark:
the moon awake and full so all the rooms
are sluiced milk-bright.
No rain for days: the rustle of a grassy land –
sometimes the wind so huge it slams the doors.

Each day seems made of birds, as though they bring
a warning in their voices that we cannot understand.
I lie awake remembering Noah and his ship –
the great sea that they rode until the land.
I think of canyons pillaged for their gold, the bears
brought out of caves on chains.
The world is left bereft of so much good
and still we do not learn, but choose
to rush towards the cliff edge, madly dancing.

BRINE

whenever we are knocked
on the jagged edges of this world
we weep pieces of the sea that once began us,
flow in streams to leave our eyes disastered –

this sea that's still inside us
so old and long ago
we can't remember:
a time before time even started being
or life on earth began

we cannot see it heals
yet when it pours across our wounds
and smooths the places that are sore
it leaves a watermark
to show the story of our sorrow
still written on our skin.

THE TWELFTH

Today there is nothing but the memory of what's lost,
like the sadness of a piano heard from a house
in early evening over a long field.
December settles into the soul and says:
This is the end. The journey is over.

One leaf clings to a tree in the garden:
the wind hurries through, searching and strange.
There are no colours left – it is as though
some provisional government in London
decreed they were illegal and banned them overnight.

A flock of birds twinkle the air and are gone,
and then it comes to me: spring is the small things
that come from the darkness, the little things
that were forgotten, that come back to cry:
There must be, there will be.

MOTHER

The house is held hard in the garden's heart;
the frost has come at last, the ground
will not be broken now for weeks and weeks.
Inside it does not smell as home once did;
the rooms have different names and everything has moved.

In the room that once was mine you lie
and when you speak so small and far away
it takes long seconds for the sound to understand.
Mother, who taught me once to love all things,
have faith now out across the water, into light.

FLANDERS

The soil was rich, thick and dark,
yet autumn after autumn he beheld the same thin harvest,
as though a shadow still lay on the land
and sunlight could not bear to blossom there.

Year on year the ploughing
turned up bones, whole shattered fragments:
dry shards of things – shins and fingers –
an eerie, brittle hoard.

One night he dreamed he worked a whole year long
to riddle through that broken field of bones,
and when he stood and looked they rose up one by one –
young men, tall and straight and fine.

And over them like slow fire crept their uniforms;
their hands and feet slid out and faces formed like wax.
They breathed, they breathed in black and white through rain,
till last of all grew guns against their sides.

And just before he woke he knew what he must do,
as each stood silent looking out at him.
He'd find their stories, he would sift each one –
the gold beneath his field.

BOXING DAY

And now the day is passing and through grey, wet light
the first homes shine out orange and the trees turn slowly
                                                    black;
and all along the valley Christmas traffic slushes north,
as the church bell echoes seven and the sleet begins to fall.

I sit beside the window and gaze out across the fields,
at the misting of the dusk as hills slide upwards into sky.
The cathedral locked in silence with the river like a shroud;
not a single sound of birdsong as the day begins to die.

Mrs James is in her rectory, alone another year;
her neighbours all left widows, and their lot the same as hers.
That loneliness I sense beats like a nerve of dull, dark pain;
it aches against my forehead at the falling of the night.

And all of us are journeying, by different lights and many roads;
and some of us have passengers, though most are lonely and
                                                    afraid.
For we never show our faces to the others that we meet,
only hiding in our silence till the years have slipped away.

We fill the days with pleasures and we try to laugh at time;
we talk and travel, read and watch, and do a thousand things.
Yet we can't quite fill the vacuum at the end of every day,
when we go to close the curtains and there's nothing left inside.

SPOUTWELLS

That December the cold stood still –
skies not blue but white;
branches, traced pale with veins of snow
cracked sometimes, broke and fell.

We left food for the deer on the far side of the fence;
they came so close we sensed their breath
before they scattered, soft as snowflakes
back into the vastness of the woods.

Sometimes I braved the track of ice
up deep into the hills. The ponds were blind white eyes;
it was as though the birds had gone, all flown –
I stood in painted silence.

THE SWANS

One spring morning, five years old
she'd opened the curtains on her own
to the opalescence of the skies.
She dressed and danced the path to the lake;
and there at the water's edge her father,
his empty body left beside the lake for ever,
the swans dipping and furling – snow shapes, soundless.

She looked out all those long years later
on the winter of her life.
The sleet came in thick wet lashes
turning the hillsides somewhere between green and grey,
a milky film across the water.

She went about the everydayness of her life:
rubbled coal into the scuttle,
put clothes on the line as always.
Yet everything was about trying to forget;
all of it about the day she'd taken the path to the lake
and run back with that light all lost,
the snow left frozen like a snowball in the sky.

Until that morning the swans came back,
their wings beating big enough to hear –
stretched into the unruffled lake.
She took the path brittle and bent, the bread in her hands,
and as she fed them she broke, slowly, piece by piece,
and the crying that tore her shoulders
was good and beautiful – a kind of song.

THE TWO

This morning early the mother and her cygnet
crossing the dark water underneath my window
in among the meltings of last night's ice.

The wind-still trees all lifeless, leafless –
the road above just thrashing traffic –
a hurry that does not touch or hurt them.

The cygnet fluffed with brown and downy,
not broken yet into the whitest snow –
sculpted out of silence both.

AUTUMN

I opened the door into the wood and listened:
through the low wool of the mist
the last leaves dwindled like dancers
down to a golden floor.

It was me that broke the silence:
my boots splintered one twig
so the whole wood shook and rattled with wings –
the roe deer froze, their eyes all glazed.

Everything listened then –
the silence a waiting, the quiet a watching;
until my feet had disappeared, my shadow passed –
and only the rain fell still, in soft glass beads.

NOTHING

There are days when nothing happens at all:
it is October and the thick scent of peat
is tugged out of chimneys in scarves.

The sea has nothing big or beautiful to do
but lie somewhere between green and blue
under the muffled light of the sun.

And I am going to Columba's Bay
by boulders and broken paths
and when I get there I will do nothing but listen.

LEARNING

Somewhere it dripped, time ticked –
every second seemed dissected.
One of twenty something sculptures out of white,
toes touching the polished rim,
I shivered thin and white –
the whole place made of coldest stone,
carved from marble a hundred years before.

Far away at the deep-end the master paced
raging about inter-house galas and the falling of
                                                    birthdays.
I listened and swam away, to somewhere
far beyond the silliness of this, to somewhere
I was free. I never heard my own surname
sworn at; I didn't see his face
hating my own, the air sore with shouting.

EASTER

I

As though I woke up in my dreaming
and opened the window wide –
to the morning scent of lemons
and the promise of newborn light.

But three shadows fell from the hill,
grew out of the ground like trees;
and I felt the agony of feet and hands
that ran from them in rivers.

I closed the window tight once more
for I could not bear to see –
and you came towards me, grey and bare,
leaving footprints of fresh blood.

II

That beautiful night the silence
as they went out to pray.
What was there to fear
in the hushed trees and scented night?

Why should they pray?
Was it not enough to listen to the starlight;
lie easy at last
in the blissful nothingness of grass?

The hungry nights behind them
and days of endless crowds;
the barefoot miles for bread
and broken promises of wells.

Had they come this far
to keep on praying?
Did not God hear their hearts
in the blessing of blissful rest?

It was his crying woke them.
They watched him against the sky
as though he tried to find a way out
of the agony of himself.

III

What did you want from him really?
What had you expected? The miracle of an army
conjured from scorched earth, marching against Rome
to bring the eagle down? He must have
burned in your hands, his turning of love
out of baskets of anger and hate. You knew in the end
he was walking to his own death, wished it on himself.
So you sold him. What was it that you wanted?
Your belly sore with three years of hand to mouth;
the quick crust here under a netful of stars
as the dogs began to bark morning; the sudden gush
of cool water in the dizzy blue thirst of the day.
You missed things: you lay awake in the cold forlornness
thinking of what had been, wondering if it was all mad;
a dry and dusty road leading to a dead end.
So you sold him. One afternoon, your head sweet with
                                                    wine,
you made up your mind. You found your feet
slipping among the stones; you went through a low
                                            doorway
and told them. Their faces white as bread, ovals
watching you, unable to believe the echo of the words.
You went back then, sat under his words still
as if nothing had happened, and his shadow
fell on you every time, heavy, huge, a hurt in the eyes

as though he knew already. You lay at night
and the drum of your heart pounded the darkness awake;
the secret burned like a worm beneath your skin.
What had you done? What had he done to you
to deserve this? You woke tired, carrying the stone of
                                        your guilt
until it killed you too.

IV

Irony nails you
the carpenter
to a wooden cross

V

All day under the circling,
the golden hugeness of the sun
beat by beat the maddening, terrible day
the terrible madness until, suddenly, at last
the sky went ugly with bruises, a thunder stuttered
in the red hills and the rain came hard as grapes
heavy, hissing, huge, and lightning gouged the dust.
His face, she saw his face, her son
the son she'd brought into a stable
shining with bright rain and blood in rivers
and how his head slipped forwards, finished,
his shoulders torn like wings, like angel wings
broken now for ever by the weight
of this last loss of God.
But even then they waited, the soldiers and the priests
watching him with gaping mouths as if they still expected
he might speak or heal or teach.
They watched the rain shine his shoulders and his broken
                                                            head
hour after hour after hour
as if they feared him still.

VI

I have crucified men
for the theft of a few coins –
I've not grown soft.
It was when he turned his head,
the nail against his flesh,
almost as though he seemed
sad at what they did.
And when they raised him high at last,
those eyes came still,
following, always following.

I have been many places
and committed crimes for Rome
I hardly knew were in my hands.
I feel no guilt.
Yet that man follows me:
I see his face in every journey, watching;
looking at me as he did that day.
I wonder who he was.

VII

Nothing. All through the night
listening and locking doors, whispering
just in case. Shadows
ghosting the streets, the gnaw
of hunger. The going over and over
the ashes of the days, searching
for something that might make sense.
No star in the sky, no light –
just the wound of morning in the end,
before remembering, before trying to pray
in the empty silence of the walls
and feeling all the words like dust
scattered and blown away.
The slow beat of time, hour by hour
like drops of blood, like drops of grief
till night and sleepless dark.

VIII

She had not slept for days.
She had forgotten food.
She barely knew her name.
Just lay and listened to the city sleep.

She went because she did not know what else to do.
She did not care or think which path she took;
if they should find her now what could they do:
the one she'd served and loved was dead.

A green star on the sky's far edge
and a single bird sang darkness bright.
She found her way: would watch, keep vigil
until they came to chase her off.

She crouched so small so long
the cold crept sore through hands and feet.
Then somewhere on the eastern sky
a wound that opened like a window
and from it poured a broken light
that filled the valley red.

She saw the stone was gone, the body gone –
that even here they could not grant him peace,
and through her tore an iron grief
as though beneath deep water.

She saw in fragments that a man
stood there before her – doubtless come to mock
and from her poured a waterfall of words
that flowed into the uselessness of grief.

Only when he swam before her
and filled her empty eyes
did she fit together all the fragments of his voice
and hear her own name whole and new again.

IX

It was over. They left Jerusalem in the dead of night;
no light alive, the grey rocks of the last days
raw and jagged in their throats.
They were fishermen; went back, broken
to the only thing they knew, to Galilee.

And all night nothing;
the skies aubergine, a piling of bruised clouds,
the lake eerie and moonless, creeping with shadows;
the cold leaking into feet and hands like leprosy.

Dawn was a wound in the east, a gash,
the twist of a rusted knife.
And there a figure on the shore beside a fire;
someone who seemed to wait for them.
They drudged up the boats, deep into dry sand.
He spoke to them with his eyes,
gave them pieces of smoky fish.

They knew him when he called them by their names.

X

Are you sure? he asked.
Quite certain. The marks
are there without a doubt.
See for yourself.

That night they were there
close around one candle.
He came through a door,
gathered among them.

Doubt forced him forwards
to touch the dark void
of all the missing points –
he believed in nothing.

WAY

If I were to touch his feet
I would feel the journey
that took three years to live
three days to heal.